A Life in Pictures
Rihanna

Emily Clark

Trans
Atlantic
Press

'I wanted to do what I had to do, even if it meant moving to America.'

From Barbados to America

Opposite: When Robyn Rihanna Fenty was only 15 she formed a group with two other girls and auditioned for veteran producer Evan Rogers, who was immediately struck by her talent and stage presence. Two years later, at the beginning of 2005, she had a recording contract with Def Jam Recordings and had moved from her home on the Caribbean island of Barbados to live with Evan and his wife in Connecticut. She later told *Entertainment Weekly*, 'When I left Barbados, I didn't look back. I wanted to do what I had to do, even if it meant moving to America.' She spent the following three months working on her debut album, *Music of the Sun*, which was released in August 2005. Her debut single, 'Pon de Replay', which was also released in August, reached No.2 on the *Billboard* Hot 100 and made it into the Top Ten in 16 other countries around the world.

Right: Rihanna performing at the Teen People Listening Lounge hosted by Jay-Z at the Key Club on July 14, 2005, in West Hollywood, California.

Music of the Sun

Many of the tracks on *Music of the Sun* were inspired by Rihanna's Caribbean roots, mixed with R&B, pop and reggae. The album received mixed reviews from the critics; Jason Birchmeier of Allmusic said it 'descends into faceless slow jams after a while, overall consistency not being among its attributes, but thankfully it picks up the pace toward the end... the result is one of the more engaging urban dance-pop albums of the year'. Despite the critics the album was commercially successful, staying in the US charts for 35 weeks and being certified Gold in the UK and US, and Platinum in Canada only four months after its release.

Above: Teairra Mari, Jay-Z and Rihanna answer questions at the Jay-Z Hosts Teen People Listening Lounge at the Canal Room in New York City on July 20, 2005.

Opposite: Rihanna performing on MTV's *Total Request Live* in New York City on September 6, 2005.

'2005 taught me the dedication and responsibility it takes to make this dream into a reality'

On tour with Gwen Stefani

To promote her first album Rihanna went on tour with Gwen Stefani towards the end of 2005, appearing as a guest artist. She said later that this had introduced her to rock music and had changed her perspective on her own work. Early the following year she also appeared in a Nike music video, which featured her new song 'SOS'. She told reporters, 'I'm actually their first artist to endorse the brand, 'cause they always have athletes. And that surprised me when they asked me, I was like, "What?! You want me?" It's fun, I really enjoy working with them, they're great people.'

Above: On stage during a MTV Networks Tempo Channel launch event at the Plantation & Garden Theater in Christ Church, Barbados, on October 22, 2005.

Opposite: Rihanna and singer/songwriter Chris Brown in December 2005. It was not long before the two young stars began a relationship that was to last for several years.

'A *Girl Like Me* is a more personal album... *Music of the Sun* was more of a party album'

Left: Rihanna attends Beyoncé's birthday and record release Party for her new album *B'Day* at the 40/40 Club in New York in September 2006. Rihanna had released her third single, 'SOS', in March 2006 and it was her biggest commercial success to date, reaching No.1 in the *Billboard* Hot 100, Hot Dance Club Play and Pop Songs charts, as well as the Australian and European charts. To support the single and her first album she had also embarked on her first headlining tour, Rihanna: Live in Concert, which opened in San Francisco in June 2006 and travelled around North America, finishing in St Louis in September 2006. In October she also played three concerts in Australia on Jay-Z's Roc tha Block tour, which also featured Ne-Yo.

Above: Rihanna performs at the Pussycat Dolls concert at the Point Theatre in Dublin, Ireland, on November 24, 2006. She had joined the Pussycat Dolls as a special guest from November 2006 to February 2007 on their tour of the UK, not long after finishing her own tour of North America. Less than eight months after her debut album, Rihanna had also released her second studio album, *A Girl Like Me*, which topped the charts in Canada and reached the Top Five in five other countries, including the US and the UK. It went on to be certified Platinum in five countries, and double Platinum in Canada and Ireland.

A Girl Like Me

Performing during the World Music Awards 2006 Show at Earls Court in London in November. In August Rihanna had made her debut as an actress, playing herself in a cameo role in the cheerleading movie *Bring it on: All or Nothing*, which was very successful as a video release. Around this time she also got her first tattoo, a couple of tiny music notes on the inside of her right foot near the ankle. It was the first of many – she said in an interview, 'I like hanging out in tattoo shops. I am so intrigued by tattoos. It's an entire culture, and I study it. Sometimes I go with friends, or just by myself. I get bum-rushed, but I don't care. I don't take security.'

It was also in 2006 that Rihanna founded the Believe Foundation, which aims to inspire and protect children in need all over the world by providing educational, financial, social and medical support when and wherever it is needed. In particular, the foundation raises awareness of the impact of blood cancers and works to recruit new bone marrow donors.

Rihanna's Believe Foundation aims to inspire and protect children in need all over the world

'a promising young vocalist growing into her own'

Unfaithful

'Unfaithful', the second single from *A Girl Like Me*, was released in June 2006 and was an even bigger international hit than Rihanna's previous singles, reaching the Top Five in fifteen countries, the Top Ten in another four, and hitting No.1 in the US, Canada, Hungary and Switzerland. A review of 'Unfaithful' in *Billboard* magazine said: 'she effectively conveys the struggle of a woman desiring to end her disloyal ways... the song ultimately reveals a promising young vocalist growing into her own.'

Opposite and above: Rihanna with director Anthony Mandler on the video shoot for 'Unfaithful' in March 2006.

Good Girl Gone Bad

In May 2007, Rihanna released her third studio album, *Good Girl Gone Bad* – and a review in UK newspaper the *Sun* of her concert at Wembley in December 2007 was headlined: 'Rihanna Going Bad is Very Good'. Reviewer Larry Meyler went on to say, 'With stage presence to match a pre-meltdown Britney and moves that would have Beyoncé quaking in her hot pants, Rihanna blew the roof off a sold out Wembley last night. The Barbadian beauty shook off any "teen pop" image as she rocked the stage in a charged set with powerhouse vocals and numerous black bondage outfit changes… The singer certainly proved that she can hold her own against any of the mega female stars out there with an explosive live show.'

Above: Rihanna performs during the live broadcast of the German TV show *Wetten, dass…?* in Leipzig on November 10, 2007, and (opposite) in concert in Dublin, December 2007.

'Rihanna
going bad is
very good'

Rihanna's umbrella

Chris Brown and Rihanna perform during the
2007 MTV Video Music Awards in Las Vegas on
September 9, 2007. They performed a medley
of 'Wall to Wall', 'Umbrella' and 'Kiss, Kiss' and
danced to 'Billie Jean'. Rihanna also picked up an
award that evening: she received the Video of the
Year Award and Monster Single of the Year – both
with Jay-Z – for 'Umbrella'. The single had been
released in March 2007 and had been a great
commercial success, hitting the No.1 spot in 13
countries and making it to the Top Five in all the
others. It stayed at No.1 for nine weeks in the UK.

Rihanna invited Justin Timberlake, Ne-Yo, Timberland and Tricky Stewart to work with her on *Good Girl Gone Bad.*

'Now I'm in complete control of my image and everything else. It takes time. You learn.'

Opposite: Rihanna and Ne-Yo performing 'Hate That I Love You' during the 2007 American Music Awards in Los Angeles on November 18, 2007. The single had been released that August to generally good reviews: BBC Music called it 'a gorgeously simple modern duet'. Rihanna won Favourite Female Artist in the Soul/R&B category that evening – at the time she was touring Europe on her massive Good Girl Gone Bad tour and had returned between concerts especially for the event. The tour had begun in Vancouver in September 2007 and covered 19 dates in North America, before moving on to Europe and concerts in 19 different countries. It then covered Asia, Africa and Oceania throughout 2008 before closing in Mexico City in January 2009.

Above: Beyoncé and Rihanna in 2007. Earlier that year Rihanna had cropped her long hair short and dyed it black – she told a reporter from the *Guardian* newspaper, 'At first I just took what was given to me, but eventually I started saying "no". I said, "I don't wanna wear that and I wanna wear my hair like this." Now I'm in complete control of my image and everything else. It takes time. You learn.'

Rihanna with Morris Day of The Time on stage at the 50th Annual Grammy Awards at the Staples Center in Los Angeles on February 10, 2008. The golden anniversary of the ceremony featured several performances from modern artists paired with stars from the past – The Time had re-formed especially for the event.

Right: Jay-Z and Rihanna accept the Best Rap/Sung Collaboration award onstage for 'Umbrella', from her album *Good Girl Gone Bad*, during the 50th Annual Grammy awards. As CEO of Def Jam Recordings, Jay-Z had been responsible for Rihanna getting her record deal in the first place – Rihanna said later, 'The audition definitely went well. They [Def Jam] locked me into the office – till 3am. And Jay-Z said, "There's only two ways out. Out the door after you sign this deal. Or through this window ..." And we were on the 29th floor. Very flattering.'

'*Good Girl Gone Bad* was the perfect title because it showed people I'm my own person now'

Nineteen awards

Opposite: Rihanna and Chris Brown perform on stage during Z100's Jingle Ball at Madison Square Garden in New York City on December 12, 2008. The year had been good for Rihanna: she had won six music awards in her home country of Barbados, two American Music Awards, seven *Billboard* awards – including Female Artist of the Year, a Grammy, two MuchMusic Video Awards, and the NRJ Music Award for Best International Song.

Left: Rihanna first had a few stars tattooed on the nape of her neck in Los Angeles, which were later extended into a river of stars flowing across her upper back. She also added a Sanskrit prayer down her right hip, an Arabic phrase across her ribcage and various motifs on her fingers and hands – including 'Shhh' on her right index finger.

A river of stars

End of a relationship

Rihanna and Chris Brown at the 2009 Grammy Salute to Industry Icons honouring Clive Davis at the Beverly Hilton Hotel on February 7, 2009. The following day the two stars were scheduled to perform at the main 2009 Grammy Awards ceremony, but in the early hours of the morning they had a row, and Chris Brown was later charged with assault. Although they apparently made up after the incident, a restraining order meant Brown had to stay at least 50 yards away from Rihanna – except at industry events, when it was 10 yards – despite a request from Rihanna's lawyer for a less restrictive order. It was not long before their relationship was reported to be over.

Rated R produced five hit singles, including 'Russian Roulette', 'Rude Boy' and 'Te amo', and the US releases 'Hard' and 'Wait Your Turn'

Rated R

Rihanna's fourth studio album, *Rated R*, was released in November 2009; it was musically miles away from her previous album, much darker and more mature. Many believed this was as a result of what had happened in her relationship with Chris Brown, although none of the songs on the album directly referred to the incident. In a review *Rolling Stone* magazine said, 'Rihanna has transformed her sound and made one of the best pop records of the year.' It was not only critically acclaimed but also commercially successful – in the UK it was certified Gold after only being on sale for four days.

Opposite: Rihanna with good friend Katy Perry in 2009, and (right) browsing in the Chanel shop in Los Angeles.

Rihanna
Entertainment

In 2010 Rihanna launched a new company, Rihanna Entertainment, to oversee all her businesses, including music, film, fragrance, fashion and book ventures. Her coffee table book, called *Rihanna*, was published in October 2010; it contained backstage photographs and other images from Rihanna's life during the creation of her album, *Rated R*.

Earlier in the year Rihanna was named International Female Artist of the Year at the 2010 NRJ Music Awards at MIDEM, held in Cannes, France. The same month she was also awarded Song of the Decade for 'Umbrella' at the Barbados Music Awards, as well as being named Entertainer of the Decade. During the year she continued to develop musically, collaborating with other artists such as Eminem, Kanye West, Canadian rapper Drake and Britney Spears. Here she is pictured with Eminem at the MTV Video Music Awards in 2010.

'Entertainer of
the Decade'

Controversy with Eminem

Rihanna is featured singing the chorus on Eminem's song 'Love the Way You Lie' – released in August 2010 – which has a theme of abusive relationships. It was immediately assumed that this referred to both Rihanna's and Eminem's personal lives, although when American singer/songwriter Skylar Grey wrote the original lyrics she had apparently been thinking more of relationships within the music industry. The video shows actors Dominic Monaghan and Megan Fox playing out a failing relationship while Rihanna and Eminem perform the song; it caused considerable controversy because of the graphic depictions of domestic violence. Director Joseph Khan, who wrote the script, said: 'We wanted to make a specific story about two people ... not a video that was representative of all couples or all domestic violence situations ... I just want people just to be able to identify with the characters and recognize that they've seen relationships like this where two people are together that are completely wrong for each other and things spiral out of control.'

Opposite: Rihanna at Nickelodeon's Annual Kids' Choice Awards in 2010, and (left) spotted on location for a music video on the Lower East Side of Manhattan in September 2010.

'We've never done a tour to this capacity. The production is unbelievable and the costumes, we just took it to a whole new level. Visually and sonically it's going to be a big step up from the last time.'

Last Girl on Earth

The Last Girl on Earth tour began in April 2010, opening in Antwerp, Belgium, and moving through 15 countries in Europe on the first leg. The second leg covered North America, beginning in July 2010 and running until the end of August. Rihanna then took a six-month break before starting the final leg in Australia in February and March 2011. She had told fans to expect a tour that was much more spectacular than her previous tours, and she certainly succeeded: the *Telegraph* newspaper review of her opening night concert in England said, 'Rihanna has a set full of hits and each is delivered with maximum bang for the audience's bucks, with revealing costumes, salacious dance routines, eye-catching props and sci-fi screens.'

Right: Performing in Las Vegas during the Last Girl on Earth tour. In 2007 Rihanna's legs were insured for $1 million by Gillette, after they named her 2007 Celebrity Legs of a Goddess. She told a reporter at the time, 'I think I'm just normal ... "Do people really insure their legs for a million dollars?" If it was my million dollars, I'd probably walk about in pants all day long.'

Loud flirts and struts with joy.

A change of management

Rihanna, Juelz Knowles and rapper Jay-Z onstage during the 52nd Annual Grammy Awards in 2010. Rihanna announced that she had split with manager Marc Jordan and joined Jay-Z's Roc Nation Management.

In November 2010 Rihanna released her fifth studio album, *Loud*, which shot straight to No.3 on the *Billboard* 200 chart. It reached No.1 in the UK charts and went on to become one of the major sellers of the year, even though it had only been released in the final months of the year. It was much more exuberant in tone than her last album, leading most critics to give it a favourable review; the *New York Daily News* said, 'Rihanna's new disk is a thrilling refutation of her previous *Rated R*. Where that disk brooded with dark rhythms and dire pronouncements, *Loud* flirts and struts with joy.

'Exploding on stage in a neon-tuned bubble, the Barbadian singer delivered an enthralling performance that never let up.'

The Loud tour to support the album began in June 2011 in Baltimore and zigzagged across the world. The first leg covered North America, finishing in early August, then 10 days later Rihanna was in Europe for a short run. September saw her in South America, then back in Europe again for a much longer run that only finished just before Christmas. In all she played 98 concerts over 21 different countries in the space of 7 months, grossing $90 million. The Scottish newspaper the *Daily Record* reviewed the Glasgow concert: 'R&B superstar Rihanna blew the roof off Glasgow's SECC last night with her aptly-titled Loud tour. Exploding on stage in a neon-tuned bubble, the Barbadian singer delivered an enthralling performance that never let up.'

Opposite: Rihanna at the 2011 *Billboard* Music Awards in Las Vegas, in May, and (right) at the Rio Festival in September 2011.

Never a failure, always a lesson

Above: Rihanna attending the Alexander McQueen: Savage Beauty Costume Institute Gala at the Metropolitan Museum of Art in New York City on May 2, 2011. The tattoo on her right shoulder had been done in December 2009, in New York tattoo parlour East Side Ink; it's her own personal motto, 'Never a failure, always a lesson', tattooed backwards so she can read it in the mirror. Tattoo artist Bang Bang said, 'I asked her why she wanted that and she said, "It's kind of my motto in life for everything. Instead of considering things to be mistakes, considering them lessons." She said that she wanted to do it in grey, rather than black, because she wanted it to be more subtle. She didn't want it to draw too much attention.'

Opposite: A candid shot taken in February 2011.

Only Girl in the World

In February 'Only Girl (In The World)' – Rihanna's lead single from her album *Loud*, which had been released in September 2010 – won Best Dance Recording at the Grammy Awards in Los Angeles. A cry to a lover to be 'the only girl in the world' for him, it had been her ninth US No.1, as well as reaching the top spot in 13 other countries and the Top Five in another 11. It was quickly certified Platinum in 8 countries, twice Platinum in Switzerland, three times Platinum in the United States and a massive five times Platinum in Australia. The video was also considerably less edgy than some of Rihanna's previous offerings: it showed her alone in a series of simple but beautiful landscapes, as if she really were the only girl in the world.

Left: Rihanna performs during the half time show at the NBA All-Star Game at the Staples Center in Los Angeles in February 2011, and (opposite) at the BRIT Awards 2011 in London.

> 'Rihanna sings as if she is in love with life, and wants to bring us along for the party'

Talk That Talk

Left: Rihanna at *The X Factor Live Elimination Show* in West Hollywood in November 2011. The previous month she had appeared in the Judges' Houses round as a guest mentor with LA Reid. In November she also released her sixth album in seven years, *Talk That Talk*, which debuted at No.1 in the UK album charts and No.3 in the US. In the UK it was certified Platinum after only six days. The lead single from the album, 'We Found Love' was also at No.1 in the UK singles chart at the same time – the second time Rihanna had manage this feat in a single year, since *Loud* and its single 'What's My Name' had also held the top spots in January. The *Daily Telegraph* said that the 'demons from her relationship with Chris Brown now sound fully exorcised – Rihanna sings as if she is in love with life, and wants to bring us along for the party.'

Right: Rihanna signs autographs as she leaves her hotel in Paris, October 2011.

Rihanna performs in Zurich, Switzerland, in November 2011. The European leg of the tour closed at the O2 Arena in London at the end of December. Rihanna hit the headlines after she was spotted riding the underground line on the way to a rehearsal at the Arena – fans were delighted as she chatted to them during the journey. She may have a healthy 'girl-next-door' attitude when it comes to travel, but Rihanna is well on the way to superstardom; when 'S&M' hit the top spot on the *Billboard* Hot 100 in April 2011, she took the record for the fastest accumulation by a solo artist of ten No.1 hits in the US – and she is also the youngest artist to reach that milestone. In her career to date she has sold more than 60 million singles and 20 million albums, and holds the overall record for digital track sales in the US – which makes her one of the best-selling artists in the world today.

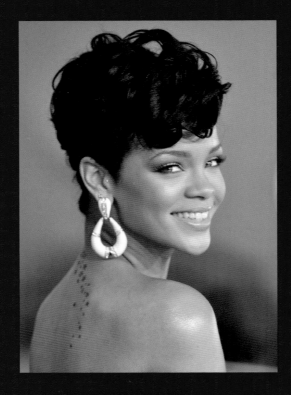

This is a Transatlantic Press book
First published in 2012

Transatlantic Press
38 Copthorne Road
Croxley Green, Hertfordshire
WD3 4AQ, UK

A catalogue record for this book is available from the British Library.
ISBN 978-1-908849-01-4

Printed in China